Red Admiral
forewing with a central reddish band and white apical spots; hindwing with a broad reddish border

1.75–2.7"

Weidemeyer's Admiral
black with a broad white spot band; ventral wing surface with extensive white and some reddish bands and bars

2.2–3.8"

3–4"

1.1–1.5"

Mourning Cloak
broad irregular yellow wing border; outer row of purplish-blue spots; dull black ventral wing surfaces with fine striations

Cinnabar Moth
forewing dull black with red leading margin and red marginal spots; red hindwing with a thin black border

1–1.3"

1.75–2"

Common Sootywing
forewing shiny black above with small white spots; hindwing mostly unmarked black

Red-Shouldered Ctenucha
shiny black narrow wings; head and forewing bases are reddish-orange; abdomen is iridescent blue; day flying; found at flowers

2.2–2.4"

Ranchman's Tiger Moth
forewings black with cream spots; hindwing orange with black spot bands; abdomen orange with black transverse bands

0.8–1.25"

Echo Azure
wings light blue above in males, females with broader dark margins; ventral hindwing whitish-gray with small dark spots

1.1–1.4"

Blue Copper
wings bright blue with thin black veins in males; females dull purplish-brown with dark spots; ventral hindwing whitish-gray and unmarked or with a few darker spots

1.4–2"

Great Purple Hairstreak
wings iridescent blue in males; dusty blue with broad black borders in females; ventral hindwing black with red spots near thorax and blue spots near two hair-like tails; reddish-orange abdomen

0.6–1"

Rocky Mountain Dotted Blue
wings blue in males, brownish in females with an orange marginal band on hindwing; ventral hindwing whitish-gray with scattered black spots and a prominent band of black-capped orange spots

0.75–1.1"

Acmon Blue
wings above blue in males, brownish in females; dorsal hindwing with an orange marginal band; ventral hindwing whitish-gray with scattered black spots and a prominent band of black-capped orange spots

0.8–1.1"

Western Tailed-Blue
wings above blue in males, gray in females; both with white fringes; ventral hindwing whitish-gray with scattered black spots and an orange crescent near a single hair-like tail

male

0.8–1.2"

0.8–1.3"

Silvery Blue
wings bright iridescent silvery blue in males; duller in females with broad dark margins; ventral hindwing brownish-gray with white-rimmed black spots

Melissa Blue
wings below whitish-gray with small black spots and a prominent black-capped orange spot band

0.85–1.4"

1–1.3"

Northern Blue
wings blue in males, brownish in females with an orange marginal band; ventral hindwing whitish-gray with scattered black spots and prominent band of black-capped orange spots

Greenish Blue
wings iridescent blue with narrow dark margins in males, females brownish with blue scaling at wing bases; ventral hindwing light gray with black spots and some light greenish scaling at base

1.1–1.3"

Arrowhead Blue
wings above blue; hindwing gray below with small black spots and larger elongated, triangular white spots

8–1.2"

0.8–1.25"

Mormon Metalmark
wings brown with orange scaling, particularly on forewing; numerous white spots

Arctic Skipper
dark brown dorsally with orange spots; hindwing below yellow-orange with dark-rimmed pale spots

1.75–2.4"

0.9–1.3"

Silver-spotted Skipper
elongated forewing; hindwing with a large white patch

Western Pine Elfin
ventral hindwing purplish-brown with irregular dark bands

1–1.5"

Tailed Copper
wings above coppery-brown; ventral hindwing gray with black spots, an irregular white band, and a small tail

1–1.4"

Common Ringlet
ventral hindwing darker brown basally, lighter tan toward margin with a pale irregular central band; ventral forewing tawny brown with paler brown apex; a small apical eyespot may be present

1.1–1.7"

1.8–2.6"

Small Wood Nymph
ventral hindwing brown with blackish-gray bark-like markings; ventral forewing with two yellow-rimmed black eyespots

Common Wood Nymph
ventral hindwing brown with darker markings and striations; ventral forewing with two yellow-rimmed black eyespots

Field Crescent
tawny orange with cream spots and black markings and borders; ventral hindwing tan with darker markings and a pale crescent spot

Northern Cloudywing
forewing with small misaligned white spots; wing fringes somewhat checkered

Common Alpine
wings dark brown with reddish orange patches enclosing numerous white-centered black eyespots

Common Buckeye
conspicuous eyespots; forewing with broad white band and orange bars; often perches on bare ground

Chryxus Arctic
light brown with black postmedial eyespots on forewing; ventral hindwing mottled black and brown with lighter markings

Lorquin's Admiral
dark brown with broad white spot band and tawny orange forewing tip; ventral wing surfaces with white and tawny orange scaling

California Sister
dark blackish-brown with a white spot band and prominent orange patch on forewing tip; ventral hindwing lighter with bluish markings

Spotted Tussock Moth
forewing tan with darker brown spots and bands; hindwing is unmarked and cream colored

Blinded Sphinx

2.2–3.6"

forewing mottled brown with scalloped margins; hindwing pinkish-brown with large black eyespot

White-lined Sphinx

2.4–3.6"

forewing with a wide diagonal white line from apex; hindwing with a pink center; feeds like a hummingbird at flowers

Columbia Silkmoth

3.1–4"

wings reddish on inner half, dull brown outer half; single central crescent spot on each wing; forewing with single dark eyespot

Ceanothus Silkmoth

3.7–5"

wings reddish-brown with paler margins; a central crescent spot on each wing, larger on hindwing; forewing with single dark eyespot

Polyphemus Moth

4–5.8"

wings above light brown; hindwing with a dark band and a single large eyespot

Dreamy Duskywing

1.1–1.5"

forewing black with heavy gray scaling and irregular bands, lacks pale transparent spots

Juba Skipper

1.2–1.6"

Wings above orange with darker markings; hindwing below tawny brown with irregular white spots

Dun Skipper

1.1–1.3"

Wings a uniformly dull, warm dark brown; forewing of female has a few small pale white spots

Common Roadside Skipper
forewing above dark brown with small apical white spots; hindwing below dark brown with violet-gray scaling on outer margin

Brown Elfin
wings above uniformly unmarked and dark brown; hindwing below reddish-brown with dark spots and an irregular dark basal portion

Bedstraw Sphinx
wings narrow and elongated; forewing olive-brown with pale central band; hindwing darker brown with pinkish-red central patch

St. Lawrence Tiger Moth
forewings dull brown with cream spots; hindwing yellow with black bands and base

0.8–1.1"

0.8–1.25"

Two-banded Checkered Skipper
dark gray with white spots and dashes; checkered wing fringes; wing bases with lighter gray hairs

Common Checkered Skipper
dark gray with prominent white spots and dashes; wing fringes are checkered

1–1.5"

3.6–5.2"

Gray Hairstreak
wings uniformly gray with a narrow black-and-white line; hindwing with an orange-capped black spot near hair-like tail; very common

Five-spotted Hawkmoth
wings narrow and elongated; wings above gray with wavy bark-like pattern; stout gray abdomen with prominent yellow spots; also known as a tomato hornworm

5–5.7"

Big Poplar Sphinx
wings narrow and elongated; forewings tan to grayish with darker bands; hindwing with a pinkish-red central patch

0.9–1.1"

0.9–1.1"

Cedar Hairstreak
variable; ventral hindwing
brownish to green with an
irregular dark outlined white
band and a single hair-like tail

Western Green
  Hairstreak
ventral forewing green with some
brown; ventral hindwing green

1–1.25"

1–1.5"

Woodland Skipper
wings above bright orange with
darker markings; hindwing tan
with a pale central spot band

Ruddy Copper
wings above a uniform bright cop-
pery orange in males; females more
muted and with darker markings

2–2.5"

1.1–1.2"

Hydaspe Fritillary
wings above orange with many
dark bands, spots on wing bases;
hindwing below violet-brown
with prominent cream spots

Mylitta Crescent
wings above orange with irregular
dark markings and paler spot
bands; hindwing below tan with
dark irregular bands

1.8–2.5"

1.75–2.6"

Green Comma
irregular wing margins; upper
side orange with darker spots
and margins; underside has bark-
like pattern

American Lady
wings above orange with dark
spots; forewing with black apex
and white spots; hindwing
below with agate-like pattern

0.8–1.35"

0.9–1.1"

Western Banded Skipper
highly variable; elongated
forewings; tawny with paler spots;
ventral hindwing pale brown with
irregular band of pale spots

European Skipper
bronze orange with dark borders,
veins darkened toward margins;
non-native; common garden visitor

Purplish Copper

wings brown with obvious purplish iridescence and black spots, females with more orange scaling; hindwing with an irregular orange band

Northern Crescent

tawny orange with black markings and borders; ventral hindwing tan with darker markings and a pale crescent spot

Pacific Fritillary

rounded wings; tawny orange with black spots and lines, darker scaling near wing bases; ventral hindwing reddish with lighter brown spots

Northern Checkerspot

reddish orange with black markings and pale central band in males; female often duller with more extensive black

Mormon Fritillary

tawny orange with black lines and spots; ventral hindwing dull orange with large silvery spots

Northwestern Fritillary

Variable; tawny with black lines and spots; wing bases darker; ventral hindwing with darker base, pale submarginal band, whitish spots

West Coast Lady

wings tawny orange with black spots; squared off forewing apex black with white spots; hindwing with band of small eyespots

California Tortoiseshell

wings tawny orange with dark borders and black spots; forewing apex squared off; irregular wing margins

1.9–2.4"

Milbert's Tortoiseshell
dark wings with wide orange band; forewing with two orange bars; forewing apex squared off; irregular wing margins

1.75–2.4"

Painted Lady
wings pinkish-orange with black spots; forewing apex black with white spots

1.8–2.5"

Satyr Comma
wings tawny with black spots and darker markings; irregular wing margins; forewing apex squared off; hindwing with short tail; ventral wing surfaces with bark-like pattern

2.6–3.3"

Viceroy
orange with black veins and borders; hindwing with postmedial black line; resembles monarch; typically found near wetlands

3.5–4"

Monarch
orange with black veins and borders; forewing with white apical spots; migratory; larvae feed on milkweeds; common garden butterfly

1.7–2.7"

Garden Tiger Moth
forewing brown with irregular white bands; hindwing orange with black-outlined blue eyespots

Mostly white

1.2–2"

Large Marble
forewing white with a black bar and a dark gray tip; ventral hindwing with an extensive yellow-green marbled pattern

1.2–2.2"

Margined White
pure white dorsally; in spring individuals have some black scaling; wings below with veins prominently outlined in gray-green scaling

1.2–2.2"

Western White
white with black checkered pattern; females more heavily patterned; intensity of dark scaling varies seasonally; open, sunny habitats

1.25–2"

Cabbage White
black-tipped forewing with black eyespot (male); two eyespots (female); non-native; garden pest of cabbage, broccoli, and cauliflower

1.6–2"

Becker's White
forewing with black spots near tip and a prominent white-centered square eyespot; ventral hindwing with yellowish veins broadly outlined in greenish scaling

1.8–2.8"

Pine White
forewing with broad black tip enclosing white spots and black scaling along leading margin; ventral hindwing with veins outlined in black

Mostly white

Stella Orangetip
forewing with a prominent black-outlined reddish-orange tip, which is smaller in females; ventral hindwing with extensive gray-green marbling

Eversmann's Parnassian
Alaska only; rounded wings; forewing somewhat transparent with gray scaling; hindwing gray with white scaling in females, pale yellow in males; hindwing with broad black inner margin and black-outlined reddish-orange spots

Rocky Mountain Parnassian
rounded wings; forewing white with black spots and gray marginal scaling; hindwing white with broad black inner margin and black outlined reddish-orange spots; females are more heavily patterned

Pale Swallowtail
large; wings white with prominent black stripes and wide black margins; forewings are somewhat pointed; hindwings with a single tail

White Underwing
forewing white with black markings; hindwing black with a broad white central band and border

Northern White Skipper
males white above with dark spots along outer wing margins; females are checkered white and gray; ventral hindwing white with tan spots

Mostly yellow

Queen Alexandra's Sulphur
1.6–2.3"
wings above with black borders in males; females with a reduced or absent black border; ventral hindwing greenish-gray with a single pale unrimmed spot

Pink-edged Sulphur
1.6–2.6"
wings yellow with a black border in males; in females border is reduced or limited to forewing; ventral forewing with silver central spot; all wings with noticeable pink fringe

Clouded Sulphur
1.6–2.7"
wings yellow with broad black border in males; females paler yellow to whitish with lighter black border; ventral hindwing with central pink-rimmed silvery spot

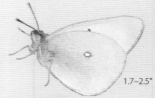

Western Sulphur
1.7–2.5"
wings bright yellow with black border in males; female paler yellow with black margin reduced or absent; ventral hindwing greenish-yellow to greenish-white with pink-rimmed central pale spot; all wings with pink fringes

Orange Sulphur
1.9–2.3"
wings above with broad black margin; ventral hindwing with a red-rimmed central spot and a dark spot band; often appears orange in flight; some females white

Old World Swallowtail
2.4–3.1"
black with yellow spots and a broad yellow central spot band; broad black wing margins with yellow spots; hindwing with blue scaling and a prominent orange eyespot near single tail on each hindwing

Anise Swallowtail
black with yellow spots and a broad central yellow spot band; broad black wing margins with yellow spots; hindwing with blue scaling and a prominent orange eyespot near single tail; eyespot with a central black pupil

Western Tiger Swallowtail
a large butterfly; prominent black stripes; broad black wing margins; each hindwing with a single tail

Two-tailed Swallowtail
a very large butterfly; forewing somewhat pointed; prominent black stripes; broad black wing margins; hindwings with two tails

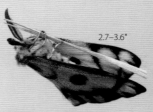

Western Sheepmoth
forewing yellow-orange with pinkish scaling; hindwing yellow-orange; both wings with black bands and a large central black spot; day flying

NOTE:
Some caterpillars possess stinging hairs or spines and can cause allergic reactions or irritation; before you handle an unidentified caterpillar, put on gloves. (Or better yet, just take pictures.) In the text below, we've called out the species where handling caterpillars may be an issue.

1.3–2.2"

2.5–3"

Silver-spotted Skipper
yellow-green with thin dark bands and a rounded, reddish-brown head

Polyphemus Moth
large; yellow-green with yellow dashes and pinkish-red spots

1.75–2"

1.5–2"

Mourning Cloak
black body with a row of crimson patches on the back, fine white speckling and several rows of black, branched spines; **spines may cause irritation**

Old World Swallowtail
green with black bands and yellow-orange spots

1–1.6"

1–1.4"

Cinnabar Moth
orange with broad black transverse bands

Painted Lady
variable; greenish-yellow to charcoal with cream mottling and rows of light-colored, branched spines

1–1.4"

1.1–1.6"

Cabbage White
green with small lateral yellow dashes and numerous short hairs

Red Admiral
variable; pinkish-gray to charcoal with lateral crescent spots and numerous branched spines

1.75-2.25"

1.75-2.25"

Garden Tiger Moth
Body covered in dense hairs; orange along the side, black hairs along the top interspersed with longer white hairs; **handling may cause skin irritation**

Spotted Tussock Moth
black at both ends with numerous white lashes; yellow abdominal band broken by black or sometimes red mid-dorsal tufts; **avoid handling**

1.2-1.6"

3-4"

Ranchman's Tiger Moth
body covered with dense long hairs, orange at the head and rear, black in the middle with scattered very long white hairs

Five-spotted Hawkmoth
bright green body with seven white stripes on the side; a prominent curved horn off the back; also known as tomato hornworm

JARET C. DANIELS, Ph.D., is a professional nature photographer, author, native plant enthusiast, and entomologist at the University of Florida, specializing in insect ecology and conservation. He has authored numerous scientific papers, popular articles, and books on gardening, wildlife conservation, insects, and butterflies, including butterfly field guides for Florida, Georgia, the Carolinas, Ohio, and Michigan. Jaret currently lives in Gainesville, Florida, with his wife, Stephanie.

Butterflies and moths organized by color for quick and easy identification

Simple and convenient— narrow your choices by color, and view just a few species at a time

- Pocket-size format—easier than laminated foldouts

- Professional photos showing key markings

- Easy-to-use information for even casual observers

- Size ranges for quick comparison and identification

- The basics of butterfly and moth anatomy

Collect all the *Adventure Quick Guides* for the Northwest

NATURE / BUTTERFLIES / NORTHWEST

ISBN 978-1-59193-937-5   **$9.95**

5 0 9 9 5

9 781591 939375

Adventure PUBLICATIONS
an imprint of AdventureKEEN